Jobs if You Like...

Sports

Charlotte Guillain

Chicago, Illinois

H **www.capstonepub.com**
Visit our website to find out
more information about
Heinemann-Raintree books.

To order:
☎ Phone 800-747-4992
💻 Visit www.capstonepub.com
to browse our catalog and order online.

Edited by Rebecca Rissman, Daniel Nunn, and
  Adrian Vigliano
Designed by Steve Mead
Picture research by Elizabeth Alexander
Originated by Capstone Global Library
Printed and bound in China by South China Printing
  Company

16 15 14 13 12
10 9 8 7 6 5 4 3 2 1

Library of Congress Cataloging-in-Publication Data
Guillain, Charlotte.
  Sports / Charlotte Guillain.
    p. cm.—(Jobs if you like...)
  Includes bibliographical references and index.
  ISBN 978-1-4329-6812-0 (hb)—ISBN 978-1-4329-6823-
6 (pb) 1. Sports—Vocational guidance—Juvenile
literature. I. Title.
  GV734.G85 2013
  796.023—dc23   2011031932

Acknowledgments
We would like to thank the following for permission
to reproduce photographs: Alamy pp. 12 (© Image
Source), 17 (© Jim West); Corbis pp. 5 (© Ocean), 6
(© Erik Isakson/Blend Images), 7 (© Stock Foundry/
Design Pics), 8 (© Ken Seet), 9 (© Image Source), 13
(© Ocean), 15 (© Image Source), 16 (© JLP/Jose L.
Pelaez), 21 (© Caterina Bernardi), 22 (© Paul Buck/
epa), 24 (© Xu Jiajun/xh/Xinhua Press); Getty Images
pp. 11 (David Cannon), 19 (Chris Polk/FilmMagic), 20
(Simon Bruty/Sports Illustrated), 25 (Stan Badz/ US PGA
TOUR), 27 (Rich Pilling/MLB Photos); Photolibrary pp.
4 (Ron Nickel/Design Pics Inc), 18 (Vladimir Godnik/
Fstop), 23 (EPA/John G. Mabanglo), 26 (Klaus Rose/Das
Fotoarchiv/Doc-Stock); Shutterstock pp. 10 (© Ipatov),
14 (© Andresr).

Cover photo of a coach with girls football team
reproduced with permission of Getty Images (John
Giustina/Iconica).

Every effort has been made to contact copyright
holders of material reproduced in this book. Any
omissions will be rectified in subsequent printings if
notice is given to the publisher.

Contents

Some words are shown in bold, **like this**. You can find out what they mean by looking in the glossary.

Why Do Sports Matter?

Do you love playing sports? Or maybe you enjoy watching sports? Even if it's not your favorite activity, sports are important for all of us. Exercise keeps us fit and healthy and can help us to relax and enjoy ourselves.

Exercise is a great way to have fun.

Teaching people to swim is just one job in sports.

If you like exercising, then you might like to get a job that involves sports. Read this book to find out about some great sports jobs. Could one of them be for you?

e a Sports Coach

If you were a sports coach, your job would be to teach people how to exercise safely and play well. Some sports coaches work with children who are learning a sport. Other sports coaches work with **professional** athletes.

Sports coaches need to help a team work together.

Athletes need coaches to help them get better at a sport.

Sports coaches help people to stay fit and learn the skills they need for a sport. They make sure people know the rules and play a game fairly. Coaches also help to **motivate** people. They tell people when they are doing well and what they can do to improve.

Be a Sports Psychologist

If you were a sports psychologist, your job would be to look at how sports change the way people think and feel. You would work with a team or athlete and help them to play or **perform** better.

Sports psychologists help athletes stay calm and focused so that they can win a race.

Sports psychologists can help sportsmen and women stay calm when they have to do a lot of training. They help to keep people positive if they are injured. Sports psychologists help people to set new goals and work toward them.

Sports psychologists can work with a team to help them win.

Be a Sports Equipment Designer

If you were a sports **equipment** designer, you would look at ways to make equipment better and safer. Some designers make swimwear that helps people swim faster. Others design snowboards that win competitions and look great!

New snowboards are being designed all the time.

This cyclist's helmet helps him to ride faster.

Sports equipment designers usually **specialize** in one sport. They might use science to understand how equipment can make someone faster. They use computers to help them design new gear.

Be a Personal Trainer

If you were a personal trainer, you would help people to exercise and become fit. You would work out a special training program for a person and help him or her to follow it.

Personal trainers push people to exercise more than they did before.

Personal trainers encourage and support people as they exercise.

Personal trainers have to get to know each person they work with. They make sure their training program is right for them. They might give people advice on food and health.

Be a Fitness Instructor

If you were a fitness instructor, you might work at a sports or recreation center. You would give people instructions as they exercise. Some fitness instructors teach yoga or show people how to use **equipment** in a gym.

Some fitness instructors teach aerobics or exercise classes.

14

Fitness instructors need to be fit and healthy to show people how to exercise. They need to check that everyone in their class is well enough to exercise. Fitness instructors need to be energetic and good at giving instructions clearly.

Instructors need to show people how to use gym equipment safely.

Be a Sports Development Officer

If you were a sports development officer, your job would be to make sure many people can exercise and play sports. You would talk to people who don't exercise and encourage them to get fit. You might organize new sports activities to get more people involved.

Some sports development officers organize events such as runs to get people into sports.

Sports development officers work to make sports available for everyone.

Many sports development officers work with children and young people who need to exercise. Some work with disabled people to help them take part in the sports that interest them. They have to organize a team of coaches and **volunteers**.

Be a Dancer

If you are doing well in dance classes, maybe you could be a **professional** dancer. Some dancers **perform** ballet, and others enjoy modern or ballroom dance. Some dancers work in a theater, while others dance on television or in music videos.

Professional ballet dancers have to train hard for many years.

Dance groups practice hard to make sure they move well together.

Dancers have to work very hard to stay fit, strong, and flexible. They follow a **choreographer's** instructions to learn special dance moves. Dancers have to be good at remembering their routines and working together as a team.

e un Occupational Therapist

If you were an occupational therapist, you would help people with **physical** or **mental** problems. You would suggest ways for your patients to cope with everyday life. You might use sports and other activities to help your patients feel better.

Exercise can help people recover after accidents.

Occupational therapists talk to a patient to find out what he or she needs. Then they make a program for the patient to follow. Occupational therapists help to keep their patients active and positive.

Yoga can help people with physical and mental illnesses to relax.

Be a Sports Professional

If you are very good at a sport, you might be able to do it for your job. A sports **professional** is someone who is able to earn the money they need to live by **competing** in their sport.

Only the very best athletes and players can be professionals.

Sports professionals have to spend a lot of time training. They need to eat healthy food and work with doctors and coaches to stay fit. They often have to travel to go to competitions and **perform** well under pressure.

Sports professionals have to play in front of many people.

Be a Sports Journalist

If you like watching sports, then you might like to be a sports journalist. Your job would be to watch sports competitions and report on them. You might write about sports for a newspaper or Website, or you might talk about sports on television.

Sports journalists need to talk to the people who play sports.

Sports writers have to write about a sports competition in an exciting way. They need to understand the sport very well to tell people what happened. Sports reporters on television often talk about sporting events as they are happening.

Often, sports reporters help to explain how a sport is played.

Choosing the Right Job for You

When you decide what you want to do when you grow up, don't just think about school subjects. Think about what you enjoy doing. If you like to be active every day, then maybe you could be a fitness instructor or coach.

If you like to help people, then perhaps you could be an occupational therapist. If you like writing, then you might like to be a sports journalist. There are so many exciting jobs that use sports that there is something to suit everyone.

Five things you couldn't do without sports

- Stay fit and healthy
- Watch sports on television
- Ride your bike
- Go swimming
- Dance with your friends

Sports Jo Chart

If you want to find out more about any of the jobs in this book, start here:

	Dancer	Fitness instructor	Occupational therapist	Personal trainer	
You need to:	Be an excellent dancer	Be fit and active	Be good at problem solving	Be able to see what different people need	
Best thing about it:	Doing what you love every day!	It's fun!	Helping a patient do something for themselves!	Helping people reach their goals!	

Sports coach	Sports development officer	Sports equipment designer	Sports journalist	Sports professional	Sports psychologist
Be good at **motivating** people	Be good at finding out what people need	Have good design ideas	Know a lot about the rules of sports	Be outstanding in your sport!	Be good at listening to people
Seeing your players win!	Helping people to play the sport they want!	Seeing your **equipment** help someone win!	You get to watch sports all the time!	Winning!	Helping someone to be better at their sport!

Glossary

choreographer person who plans and teaches dance steps and routines

compete take part in a competition

equipment item or items used to help someone do something

mental to do with the mind

motivate make people want to do something

perform do something in front of other people

physical to do with the body

professional doing a job to earn money to live

specialize to concentrate on one thing

volunteer person who works for no money

Find Out Mor

Ballet

www.bam.gov/sub_physicalactivity/activitycards_ballet.html

You can learn more about what it takes to be a professional ballet dancer at this Website.

Activity Calendar

www.bam.gov/sub_physicalactivity/cal_index.asp

If you're serious about exercise, you can create an activity calendar at this Website.

Sports Careers

www.bls.gov/k12/sports.htm

You can learn more about different careers in sports from this Website. Ask an adult for help if you read things you don't understand.

Fitness and Exercise

www.kids.gov/k_5/k_5_health_fitness.shtml

You can find out more about sports, exercise, and staying healthy from this Website. There are lots of ideas for fun activities.

Index